To SERVE
with All Your
STRENGTH

FRAN SCIACCA

NAVPRESS
BRINGING TRUTH TO LIFE
P.O. Box 35001, Colorado Springs, Colorado 80935

OUR GUARANTEE TO YOU

We believe so strongly in the message of our books that we are making this quality guarantee to you. If for any reason you are disappointed with the content of this book, return the title page to us with your name and address and we will refund to you the list price of the book. To help us serve you better, please briefly describe why you were disappointed. Mail your refund request to: NavPress, P.O. Box 35002, Colorado Springs, CO 80935.

The Navigators is an international Christian organization. Our mission is to reach, disciple, and equip people to know Christ and to make Him known through successive generations. We envision multitudes of diverse people in the United States and every other nation who have a passionate love for Christ, live a lifestyle of sharing Christ's love, and multiply spiritual laborers among those without Christ.

NavPress is the publishing ministry of The Navigators. NavPress publications help believers learn biblical truth and apply what they learn to their lives and ministries. Our mission is to stimulate spiritual formation among our readers.

Cover design by Jennifer Mahalik
Cover photo by FPG International
Creative Team: Jill Sciacca, Jacqueline Eaton Blakley

Some of the anecdotal illustrations in this book are true to life and are included with the permission of the persons involved. All other illustrations are composites of real situations, and any resemblance to people living or dead is coincidental.

Unless otherwise identified, all Scripture quotations in this publication are taken from the
HOLY BIBLE: NEW INTERNATIONAL VERSION ® (NIV®). Copyright © 1973, 1978,
1984 by International Bible Society. Used by permission of Zondervan Publishing
House. All rights reserved.

Printed in the United States of America

1 2 3 4 5 6 7 8 9 10 / 05 04 03 02 01 00

FOR A FREE CATALOG OF
NAVPRESS BOOKS & BIBLE STUDIES,
CALL 1-800-366-7788 (USA)
OR 1-416-499-4615 (CANADA)

For
Heather Anne
and
Havilah Joy

Contents

Introduction

Almost half a century ago, an Augustinian monk fastened his invitation to a theological debate on the door of the Castle Church in Wittenberg, Germany. Little did Martin Luther imagine that this public notice would become one of the defining documents of Western civilization. Luther's *95 Theses* are a near synonym for the Protestant Reformation.

We're grateful to Luther and the other Reformers for freeing the doctrine of salvation from its bondage of faith plus meritorious human effort. Luther seemed to clarify forever that we are "saved by grace through faith," echoing the words of the apostle Paul in his Letter to the Romans. However, as we begin the third millennium of the Christian era, evidence appears to be mounting that perhaps we're ripe for another reformation. Despite the rise of the mega-church, more U.S. churches are closing than opening each year. And Christianity increasingly is equated with conservative politics rather than compassion, mercy, and personal sacrifice. Christianity appears to be shrinking along with church membership. Why is this?

The answer, in part, may be due to a misunderstanding or ignorance on our part regarding what it truly means to be "Christian." In the words of philosopher and author Dallas Willard:

> *The most telling thing about the contemporary Christian is that he or she simply has no compelling sense that understanding of and conformity with the clear teachings of Christ is of any vital importance to his or her life, and certainly not that it is in any way essential. . . . More than any other single thing, in any case, the practical irrelevance of actual obedience to Christ accounts for the weakened effect of Christianity in the world today, with its increasing tendency to emphasize political and social action as the primary way to serve God."[1]*

God's Word repeatedly stresses to us that salvation is a complex and on-going process, not an isolated event. It involves spiritual rebirth, absolution of guilt, and the declaration that the believer is forever righteous in the sight of God. But, it also includes imparting the very life of God through the indwelling Holy Spirit. This life is described by the apostle Paul as "his incomparably great power for us who believe" (Ephesians 1:19). The Christian, once forgiven, is to be engaged in the marvelous adventure of working with God as this magnificent "incomparably great power" transforms us into the likeness of His Son.

To Serve with All Your Strength is designed to help you see and understand what the life of a genuine reborn believer should "look like" to the watching world. The indwelling Holy Spirit's desire is to empower and change you. You are to cooperate with Him in His work of making you resemble Jesus Christ more and more—a process called *sanctification*. The Spirit-empowered life is one in which success, wealth, and leadership take on new and unique definitions. It is a life characterized by transformed thought patterns, behavior, and speech. And priorities are so rearranged that we become radically different from the culture that we are bathed in. As a result, the Spirit-empowered life is a life of great influence because it is a life of great credibility.

Each chapter of *To Serve with All Your Strength* will enable you to examine an area of your life that God seeks to remodel so that it more better resembles the heart of His Son. Each chapter will challenge you to think and live outside your comfort zone. But we are called to resemble Jesus Christ, and He lived outside of the comfort zone all the time!

1. Dallas Willard, *The Divine Conspiracy* (San Francisco: HarperCollins, 1998), p. xv. (Emphasis his.)

1. NICODEMUS

Spiritual Birth: End or Means?

ABIDING PRINCIPLE   The surest sign of life is growth. If I am genuinely a Christian, others will see progress—the fruit of rebirth—in my life. If there is no fruit, there is likely no life.

> *In regeneration we pass out of death into life, but in sanctification we pass out of the self-life into the Christ-life.*

— A.B. Simpson

SNAPSHOT   We live in an age of counterfeits. Artificial plants, chrome-plated plastic, and particle board products abound. But I suspect that cheap substitutions have been a reality since Cain sought to pass off his second-class offering to God just outside the Garden of Eden! Jesus Himself understood the human propensity to substitute image for substance. His first call to faith was to His fellow Jews, who believed that they were the chosen of God simply because they were descendants of Abraham. In a clandestine conversation with one of Jerusalem's premier rabbis, Jesus dispelled this myth forever. He set the record straight regarding what it means to be a true child of God. And His words are as fitting today as they were in first-century Palestine. However, they were not God's final word on the subject of salvation. In fact, if our understanding of salvation is defined by Jesus' encounter with Nicodemus, we could become as ineffective and lifeless as most of the Jews of that day.

STUDY QUESTIONS

1. Jesus' comments to Nicodemus in John 3:3-6 are best understood in the context of Paul's statement in Colossians 2:13. What is our dilemma?

What do you understand Paul to mean by the word *dead?*

What do you understand Jesus to mean by being "born" a second time?

2. When you think of being "born again" and having "eternal life," do you tend to think in terms of your past, your present, or your future?

3. Why do we not carry around photos of ourselves as infants?

4. In Matthew 7:13-23, Jesus indirectly provides some helpful principles determining who is in the family of God and who is not. Explain what characterizes one who belongs to God, and one who does not belong to God.

Verses 13-14

Verses 16-17

Verse 18

___

Verses 21-23

___

5. Read John 15:1-8. What does Jesus point to as the clearest evidence that someone is His disciple?

___

What does this evidence prove? Why?

___

6. According to the following passages, what do Peter and Paul expect to see going on in the lives of the believers to whom they are writing?

2 Peter 3:18

___

2 Thessalonians 1:3

___

Compare these two verses with what Jesus said in John 15:1-8 about fruit being evidence of your faith.

7. Read Romans 8:5-11 and John 3:1-8 again. These passages deal with the Holy Spirit, salvation, and the true believer. Would you say there is a relationship between spiritual *growth* and being spiritually *alive*? If so, what? If not, why not?

8. Based on what you've discovered in this chapter, evaluate the following statements:

"A Christian is someone whose sins are forgiven and who is going to heaven when he dies."

"Discipleship and salvation are related, but independent of each other."

"Someone can be 'born again' but not desire to grow spiritually."

RECAP

God's Word is full of metaphors and terms relating to conversion: regeneration, rebirth, adoption, and being "born again," to name a few. In response to repentance and faith, God absolves us of our guilt, credits the righteousness of Christ to us, and gives us the Holy Spirit to indwell and empower us forever! The eternal life that He imparts is not merely the promise that we will live forever. We don't carry around photos of our infancy because they don't represent who we are today. In the same way, we should focus on our present and growing relationship with God rather than simply acknowledge the fact of our spiritual rebirth.

9. According to the following passages, what is God's ultimate goal or purpose for those who have experienced spiritual rebirth?

2 Corinthians 3:17-18

Ephesians 4:11-13

How does this happen in your life?

10. Each of the passages below isolates a characteristic of Christ's life that should exist, in increasing measure, in those who are truly reborn. Read the verses, determine the spiritual quality mentioned, and complete the following sentence.
Truly reborn Christians are those who . . .

Job 23:12; Jeremiah 15:16

Ezekiel 36:26-27

Matthew 18:21-33; Colossians 3:13

Acts 4:18-20

Hebrews 2:11-12

Hebrews 10:24-25

1 John 3:14-17

11. Describe the characteristics of the infant believers in the following passages.

1 Corinthians 3:1-3

Hebrews 5:11-14

12. According to Peter's exhortation in 2 Peter 1:5-9, what should characterize the life of the believer who is maturing in faith?

Why does Peter say that maturing is so vital?

13. Submit yourself to a spiritual check-up in light of the scriptural characteristics of the life of one who is truly reborn. Place an "X" on the line that most honestly represents where you are right now in that area.

HEART TO OBEY GOD
"dead"————infant————juvenile————mature

HEART OF PRAISE TO GOD
"dead"————infant————juvenile————mature

DESIRE TO SHARE THE GOSPEL
"dead"————infant————juvenile————mature

DESIRE FOR FELLOWSHIP
"dead"————infant————juvenile————mature

ACTIVE LOVE OF OTHER CHRISTIANS
"dead"————infant————juvenile————mature

QUICKNESS TO FORGIVE OTHERS
"dead"————infant————juvenile————mature

HUNGER FOR AND DELIGHT IN SCRIPTURE
"dead"————infant————juvenile————mature

14. Summarize what you've discovered about your spiritual health from this check-up. Honestly evaluate your strengths and your weaknesses.

15. Think about the perspective you had about spiritual growth and discipleship before you began this study. What has changed, and how should that affect your life beginning today?

16. Prayerfully review your check-up and pick the area in which you are closest to the "infant" stage. Determine one thing you can do this week to begin growing in that area. Write it down. Then share your plan with one person who will faithfully hold you accountable.

SCRIPTURE MEMORY

Paul's prayer for growth—Colossians 1:9-10
The motivation of all growth—1 John 2:5-6

2. SOLOMON

Changing One's Mind

ABIDING PRINCIPLE   The command center of human nature is the mind. In order for God to sanctify our lives by conforming us to the likeness of His Son, He must have access to our minds and freedom to use His Word to change the way we think.

> *He who will not command his thoughts will soon lose command of his actions.*

—Woodrow Wilson

SNAPSHOT   Solomon, the illegitimate son of King David by Bathsheba, is an enigma of Scripture. After the death of his father, he ascended to the throne. God appeared to him in a dream and gave him the chance to choose whatever he wished. Exercising more than a modicum of wisdom, Solomon sought more—more wisdom, that is. God was so pleased with Solomon's desire to rule with justice and discernment that He rewarded him not only with wisdom, but with an abundance of material wealth and status. God Himself declared that Solomon would have "no equal among kings." His reign as the third king of the Jews began with promise, pomp, and power. However, it halted forty years later with infanticide, infidelity, and infamy. Solomon the Wholehearted had become Solomon the Coldhearted. What is it that regulates the "temperature gauge" of the redeemed heart when it comes to God? What factors work to cool it down, and how does God keep it ablaze?

SCRIPTURE   1 Kings 3:1-14; 9:1-7; 11:1-13

STUDY QUESTIONS

1. One of Solomon's first opportunities to exercise his gift of

divine wisdom is recorded in 1 Kings 3:16-28. Read this moving story and carefully answer the following questions.

Do you see this as a story of justice or compassion? Defend your answer.

What do you think Solomon would have done if the real mother had remained silent? Explain your answer.

2. Read the story in 1 Kings 11:1-8 about women and children near the end of Solomon's reign. Chemosh and Molech were "fire gods" of the Canaanites. The shrines Solomon built consisted of hollow brass statues in which fires were stoked until the outstretched arms of the god became red hot. The Jews then sacrificed their infant children by placing them onto the idols. From the text, how do you explain the transformation of Solomon from his early days as king to what he had become?

3. What is the conditional promise God reiterated to Solomon in 1 Kings 3:13-15 and 9:4-7?

To better understand Solomon's behavior transformation, we need to go back nearly seven centuries before him, where God prophetically spoke through His servant Moses. Read Leviticus 18:21 and Deuteronomy 17:14-17. List the specific prohibitions God commanded for the conduct of the Israelites' future king.

Read 1 Kings 10:14-21,26-29, and 11:1-3. How did Solomon fare regarding these prohibitions?

4. Read Deuteronomy 17:14-15 and 18-20. Describe God's instructions for the future king of the Jews. What was he to do? Be specific and thorough.

What conclusion can be made about Solomon's commitment to God's instructions?

What do you think he failed to do?

5. The following passages reveal where God's work of sanctification faces opposition. What does each passage portray as the place where the battle begins?

Deuteronomy 6:5

Deuteronomy 13:1-3

Read Proverbs 4:23. In your own words, rewrite the verse.
(Keep in mind that Solomon wrote these words!)

Solomon began his reign as king committed to do what was
right and pleasing to God. From the Scriptures you have
studied, how would you describe what led to Solomon's
downfall?

RECAP

Wisdom has been defined as the ability to see life from God's
point of view, and to act accordingly. Solomon's life is a sermon
exposing how *not* to live. After stunning the watching world with
his insight and courage, he slowly lost his reputation and renown
as the wisest king on earth. He changed from a man of tenderness
and compassion to one of cold tyranny. Solomon's heart grew
hard because he wandered from the light of God's Word. Even
though he instructed his own son to "guard [his] heart," he failed
to do so himself! Solomon stands forever as a sobering example
of what each of us can become if we desert our post and fail to
guard our hearts. This begins when we abandon our attention to
God and His Word.

APPLICATION QUESTIONS

6. In the Old Testament, the *heart* and *mind* are nearly synony-
mous. Scripturally speaking, the heart is vital to living and growing as a believer. Read the following passages and explain what
they teach about the heart and mind. (Note: The word translated
"imagination," "motive," and "intent" in these verses is the same.
It is a beautiful Hebrew word that implies a "careful working
over" of something—like pottery or art, in some cases.)

Genesis 8:21 (NASB)

---

1 Chronicles 28:9

Jeremiah 17:9

Why do you think God places such a premium on guarding
the heart and mind?

---

7. In Romans 12:1-2, God speaks about His will and intent
regarding our minds as we are being sanctified. What is His
desired outcome for our minds, and what do you understand this
to mean? (Note: The Greek word translated "transformed" is
transliterated in English as "metamorphosis" — the process in
which a caterpillar becomes a butterfly.)

What is the inevitable result if we are negligent? (You may
want to read over your responses to question 6.)

---

8. What is the relationship between God's Word and our daily
lives according to the following verses in Psalm 119?

Verses 9-11

Verse 18

Verse 24

Verse 29

Verse 32

Verses 36-37

Verse 72

9. Read the following passages. Record what each teaches about what should be going on in your mind as you are being sanctified.

Romans 8:6

1 Corinthians 2:16

_____

Philippians 2:5-7

_____

Philippians 4:8-9

_____

Hebrews 4:12

_____

Hebrews 12:2-3

_____

10. Do you think that this "renewal" of your mind is something God can accomplish apart from steady, prolonged exposure to His Word? Why, or why not?

11. Thinking about the example of Solomon's life, what would you say is more harmful to your spiritual life: neglect of daily scriptural input, or negative input? Explain your answer.

12. Assess your own commitment to the "renewing of your mind" in terms of input. In other words, based on what is going into your mind on a daily basis, are you being *conformed*, or *transformed?* Explain by using examples.

13. What is one specific source of input in your life that contributes to your mind being "conformed to this world"? (This could be a television show, use of the Internet, or conversation with specific individuals, for example.)

What will you do to change that situation?

What is one thing you can *add* to your daily life so that you are being "transformed"? Consider memorizing a passage of Scripture from this study, or beginning a disciplined devotional life.

Write down your plan and find a friend who will hold you accountable regarding both of your intentions.

SCRIPTURE MEMORY

The process of a transformed mind—Romans 12:2
The tester of my thoughts—Hebrews 4:12

3. THE UNNAMED MAN

How Do You Spell "Success"?

ABIDING PRINCIPLE   How we measure success is the quiet captain of our lives, directing our values and evaluating our efforts. Because we can be sincere but wrong, it is essential that the purposes that guide our lives are aligned with God's purposes for us.

Wealth is like sea-water; so far from quenching a man's thirst, it intensifies it. The more he gets, the more he wants.

—Roman proverb

SNAPSHOT   The Bible is full of nameless people. They often stand in contrast to the christened people, however, only because we cannot attach a name. Lot's wife is no less important than Mary or Martha. I even suspect that in some ways, she may be more significant. Jesus encountered thousands of people during His life and ministry, most of whom remain nameless to us in Scripture: Peter's mother-in-law, the Syro-Phoenician woman, a rich young ruler, and the centurion at the cross, just to name a few. Occasionally, however, Jesus told parables about nameless people who were so typical of all humanity that His listeners no doubt filled in the stories with names of their own. One such story involved a wealthy farmer who had misdiagnosed his true condition because of a mistaken view of success. As you read the parable of this particular nameless man, make sure that the name you fill in is not *your own!*

SCRIPTURE   Luke 12:13-34

1. Read Luke 12:13-15. In this introductory exchange preceding the parable, Jesus uncovers a number of tendencies people have regarding their views of success and how they choose to live.

What motivation does Jesus address in His opening comments?

Jesus isolates a very common definition of *success* in these preliminary statements. In your own words, explain this faulty but popular definition.

Success is . . .

Do you see a relationship between your two answers to this question? Explain.

2. Read Luke 12:16-19 carefully. Jesus introduces a parable here that amplifies both the improper motivation and the false definition of success that He highlighted in His introductory comments. Unfortunately, the unnamed man in this parable is an accurate portrait of most people. Using the ideas of the unnamed man, define another view of success that accurately reflects the typical modern view. (Look carefully. There is a progression in his statements that represents stages in life.)

The modern view of success says . . .

3. When this man died, do you think his friends and neighbors considered him a success or a failure? Explain your answer.

4. If *you* had known him, would you have considered him a success or failure? Explain your reasons.

5. If people believe that the unnamed man's view of success *is* wrong, the typical reason is found in God's statements in verse 20. If this verse is the standard, explain how his thinking was wrong.

The *real* reason his view of success was wrong is actually in verse 21. Why was this man a total failure from God's perspective?

6. What do you think it means to be "rich toward God"? Give an example of a contemporary person you believe lives like this.

7. The apostle Paul possibly understood the truth of this parable better than anyone else we encounter in the New Testament. Read over his abbreviated autobiography in Philippians 3:4-14.

In what ways was Paul's early life like that of the unnamed man?

What was different about his later life?

Paul gives an explanation for the dramatic change in verses 7-8. What happened to his understanding of success, and what impact did it have on his life?

Paul's statement in verse 8, "that I may gain Christ," is best understood in light of his other inspired comments. Look at the following verses and explain in your own words what you think Paul means by "gaining Christ."

Romans 8:29

2 Corinthians 3:17-18

Galatians 4:19

Colossians 1:28

Gaining Christ means . . .

8. Define success from a biblical perspective, based on all that you have learned in this chapter. Note where your understanding has changed.

Biblical success is . . .

RECAP

The popular axiom, "He who has the most toys when he dies, wins," finds no support in Scripture. There are, however, examples of those who believed and were deceived by it, including the unnamed man in this parable. In the end, worldly emblems of success make failures out of even the best of people. True success, according to the Bible, is how closely we reflect who God wants us to be when we die. And the standard by which God makes that determination is the same for every one of us: the person of His beloved Son, Jesus.

APPLICATION QUESTIONS

9. Read Luke 12:13-21, then look at the following verses and compare the description of Jesus Christ with the unnamed man in the parable. Describe what is either present or lacking in the life of Jesus, based on each verse.

Isaiah 53:2

Isaiah 53:3

Matthew 13:54-57

Luke 8:1-3

Luke 9:58

2 Corinthians 8:9

10. Jesus takes this whole idea of success a step further. In fact, He takes it to a level we probably wish He hadn't. Look at Luke 16:15. List at least six things that are highly esteemed in our day.

11. What do our modern notions of success have to do with the life and example of Jesus and the will of God for believers as outlined by Paul in the passages you have studied in this chapter? Defend your answer.

12. Where would you place your present view of success? (Think carefully. Be honest.)

Paul ———————————————————— unnamed man

13. Where would you place the view of success that you are passing on to those under your influence (such as your spouse, children, coworkers, friends, or neighbors)?

Paul ———————————————————— unnamed man

14. Our view of success is the captain of our lives, steering our thoughts and actions onto the course that we believe will allow us to reach the highest level of the standard we have set. For this reason, behavioral changes on our part cannot produce the transformation of motive and conviction that is necessary. Review your answers to questions 12 and 13. If you see that you are more like the unnamed man, begin to pray Ezekiel 36:26-27 for your life, asking God to make this "heart transplant":

> *I will give you a new heart and put a new spirit in you; I will remove from you your heart of stone and give you a heart of flesh. And I will put my Spirit in you and move you to follow my decrees and be careful to keep my laws.*

While it is true that we cannot change ourselves from the inside out, it is also true that we can minimize or eliminate activities that contribute to a wrong view of success. What activities or things consume most of your energy, time, and thoughts? Are there any that contribute to the view of success Jesus said was "detestable in God's sight"? What can you eliminate?

What activities might be more consistent with God's goal of Christlikeness for your life? List possibilities that you could be more involved in right now. Pick one that you will use to replace one that you've chosen to eliminate. Share this with a person who will hold you accountable to follow through on this plan.

Finally, take several weeks and read through the gospel of Mark with a notebook nearby. Write down every observation you can that helps you understand more clearly and specifically how Jesus lived His life. Having a fresh mental image of what He "looked" like will assist God in His transformation of your heart by giving you a mental image of His goal for you.

SCRIPTURE MEMORY

The seriousness of our view of success—Luke 16:15
God's definition of success—Colossians 1:28

4. AQUILA AND PRISCILLA

Ministry as a Lifestyle

ABIDING PRINCIPLE   Ministry to others is not merely the prerogative of paid professionals. It is the privilege, joy, and responsibility of anyone who has truly experienced the grace of God.

There is not a single passage in the Old Testament or the New Testament where the filling of the Holy Spirit is spoken of and not connected with the testimony of service.

—R.A. Torrey

SNAPSHOT   The Bible does not contain many stories about married couples in which both play a vital role in ministry. Instead, it tends to focus on one partner or the other. We read about Peter, but never about his wife. We read about a woman named Mary whose husband oversaw Herod's household, but we know little about him. One exception is a couple we meet in the book of Acts named Aquila and Priscilla. It is interesting that of the seven times their names appear in Scripture, they are always together. And they are always engaged in ministry. Wherever they traveled, from Rome to Greece to Asia, they seemed to have one thing in mind—service to others. As they opened their hearts to people, their home became a church. While it is certainly true that they ministered consistently and continually, I suspect that they did not see themselves as "ministers." Instead, they probably saw themselves simply as Christians, growing in their knowledge of and love for God.

SCRIPTURE   Acts 18

STUDY QUESTIONS

1. Read Acts 18:1-4 and answer the following questions. (Note: Because there is no clear indication when Aquila and Priscilla became Christians, it is possible that Paul led them to saving faith sometime after they met him.)

Where did Priscilla and Aquila meet Paul, and under what circumstances?

What was it that brought Paul and this married couple together?

Use your imagination to create a short, possible scenario that explains Priscilla and Aquila's conversion to Christ after arriving in Corinth from Rome (study the passage carefully for details).

2. Read Acts 18:5-11. What would you suspect became of Paul's relationship with this married couple during the eighteen months he remained in Corinth?

3. Read the following verses and chart a short history of Aquila and Priscilla's life. (The verses are arranged in chronological order.)

Acts 18:1-2

18:3

18:5-11

18:18-22

18:24-26

---

1 Corinthians 16:19 (Paul is writing from Ephesus)

Romans 16:3-5 (Paul is writing to Rome)

---

4. Look at Paul's instructions to Timothy as a young pastor in
2 Timothy 2:2 and 3:10-17. List all the similarities you can see in
Paul's impact on Aquila and Priscilla, and on Timothy.

5. What does each of the following passages teach about ministry (where it comes from, who it is for, why it exists, and so on)?

Exodus 31:1-6

Exodus 35:34

Jeremiah 3:15

Micah 3:8

Matthew 25:14-29

Mark 8:34-35; John 12:24-25

Acts 4:31

2 Corinthians 4:5

2 Corinthians 5:17-20

---

2 Corinthians 6:3-13

Colossians 1:28-29

---

1 Peter 4:10

---

6. One of Paul's discussions of spiritual gifts and their use in ministry is recorded in Ephesians 4:11-16. Read this passage several times and answer the questions below.

List the gifts God gave to the church (that is, to believers).

What does Paul say to church leaders in verse 12?

What does Paul say to individual believers in verse 12?

What is God's ultimate goal in this cooperative process (verses 13-16)?

7. Summarize what you have discovered in this chapter about the relationship between being a Christian and being involved in the spiritual growth of others. (Review all of your responses to the previous questions before you begin.)

RECAP

It is virtually impossible to read the Bible and not see the truth that God expects His people to invest into His kingdom what He has given them, which typically involves other people. In fact, Jesus warns us that if we try to hoard what we have, we will *lose our lives.* Perhaps this is why there are so many who claim to know Christ but whose lives are characterized by an absence of joy and a presence of depression or boredom. Ministering to others is not merely a mandate to "paid professionals." It is the calling of anyone who claims to be a Christian. In fact, it is often at the intersection of our life with that of another that God does His most remarkable, joyful, and permanent work.

APPLICATION QUESTIONS

8. What do you discover from 1 Corinthians 12:4-6 about the source and strength of our ministry?

What is encouraging about this?

9. Isolate the specific type of ministry described in the verses below. Whenever possible, list modern equivalents.

Job 29:15

Job 29:16; Proverbs 31:20

Isaiah 50:4

Matthew 19:14

Matthew 25:35

Matthew 26:6

Mark 6:34

Luke 8:1-3

Acts 4:32-35

2 Corinthians 9:6-7

Colossians 4:12

Philemon 7

Hebrews 13:3

James 1:27

10. Read Mark 14:8; John 6:5-10,11; and 2 Corinthians 8:12. What important principle about your ministry today do you find in these verses?

11. Read Isaiah 58:10-11. What principle and promise about ministering to others do you find in this passage?

12. Reflect on your life as a Christian over the past month. What percentage of your time has been centered around you and your relationship with God (prayer, Bible study, fellowship, and so on)? Write the percentage in the space provided. What percentage of your time has been spent growing in your relationship with God while also meeting the needs of others (ministry)? Write that percentage in the appropriate space.

Time spent on myself _____ %

Time spent on others _____ %

13. Review your responses in this last section. What has emerged from examining your own Christian life in regard to your perspective and involvement in meaningful ministry to others?

14. If your percentage from question 12 is out of balance in favor of "self," what can you eliminate from your life so that you are not so self-focused?

What can you do to replace it with something that is focused on ministry to others? (You may need to refer to your answers to question 9 and seek advice from people doing those ministries in your church or community.)

Remember that Priscilla and Aquila learned how to minister to people by spending time with Paul, who was always ministering. Think of the people you spend time with each week. Are they moving you toward true ministry or *away* from it?

Who is someone you may need to spend *more* time with, and who is someone you need to spend *less* time with? What can you do this week to make changes?

SCRIPTURE MEMORY

The healing power of ministry—Isaiah 58:10-11
God's expectations in ministry—2 Corinthians 8:12

5. TITUS

The Reality of the "Watched Life"

ABIDING PRINCIPLE   Conversion begins as an intensely private matter involving our deepest secrets and darkest sins. But if we are growing in conformity to Christ, it must increasingly become public evidence that demands a verdict.

A genuine Christian ought to be as distinguishable amongst his fellows as is a civilized man among savages.

—Hugh McIntosh

SNAPSHOT   There is much discussion and concern among Christian leaders today about the "marginalization of religious faith." In other words, the religious faith that once was at the center of importance and distinction in our culture has increasingly been moved to the periphery of our identity as Americans. One response to this has been the effort to restore biblical faith to the center of the public square. Unfortunately, this has not halted the conflict. Paul's instructions to a struggling young pastor facing a penetrating battle of "Christ and culture" in his own day sheds much light on the relationship between the modern person's faith and the watching world.

SCRIPTURE   Titus 1:1-9; 2:1-15

STUDY QUESTIONS

1. Look at the Bible's detailed specifications for a church leader in Titus 1:6-9. List the characteristics that are visible and open to scrutiny and put them under the "Public" heading in the following chart. List those that are personal or hidden under the "Marginal"

heading.

Public   Marginal

Look at your lists. Do you see any significance in the fact
that one is longer than the other? Explain.

---

2. In Titus 2:1-10, Paul instructs Titus in what he is to teach the
various groups in his churches on the island of Crete. Under
which of the headings in your chart would you place the things
Titus is to teach, and why?

Paul insists that Titus is to charge his church members to
live notable public lives. Why is this so important, according
to Titus 2:5,8, and 10?

---

3. Describe a "blameless" person.

The word blameless comes from a word family that connotes "calling someone to account" or "finding flaws." Why do you think Paul insisted that a church leader be blameless?

Read Romans 2:17-24. Paul is speaking to Jews in this passage, but what principle can you see here regarding your own lifestyle as a person professing to know Christ?

4. According to the following passages, why is it important that Christians lead blameless lives?

Philippians 2:14-16

Titus 1:16

Titus 2:3-5

5. In the following passages, Paul connects our standing before God (justification) and our spiritual growth before people (sanctification). In your own words explain Paul's main point regarding justification and sanctification in each passage.

Philippians 2:12-15

Titus 2:11-14

Why do you think God links the two?

6. Is it legitimate for people to have "expectations" of professing Christians that they do not have of other people? (Defend your answer based on what you have studied so far in this chapter.)

Do you see this as oppressive and legalistic, or reasonable and rational? Explain.

RECAP

In the first chapter we discovered that genuine spiritual birth results in spiritual growth. In this chapter we've learned that our own spiritual growth is on display to the world around us. As disconcerting as this may be, it is simply a reality that cannot be dodged or minimized. You are being watched! As the culture around us spirals away from God, being blameless simultaneously becomes more noticeable and significant. Even though you might prefer to have the world be more accepting of Christianity in general, the truth is, the world is watching you in particular!

APPLICATION QUESTIONS

7. Look up the following passages. Keep in mind the issue of your life being watched by the world around you. What additional insights can you gain about:

The importance of Christian unity? (John 17:20-23; in your answer, consider the implications of believers *not* being united.)

Credibility and effectiveness in ministry to others? (1 Thessalonians 2:9-12)

The power to become blameless? (1 Thessalonians 5:23-24; 2 Peter 1:3)

8. God pushes the principle of the "watched life" to limits we most likely wish He hadn't. Look up the following Scriptures and summarize what you see in each of them regarding this idea.

Luke 6:40,46

1 Corinthians 11:1

Ephesians 5:1

1 Thessalonians 1:6-7

9. Ponder the following questions and then answer them honestly.

Who are *you* imitating?

Is your model imitating Christ?
☐ yes
☐ no
☐ I hadn't thought about it

Who is imitating *you?*

Are you imitating Christ?
☐ yes
☐ no
☐ I hadn't thought about it

What needs to change, and what will you do about it? (This may involve ending or moving away from relationships that are discrediting the gospel. It may mean establishing new relationships with believers who are seeking to imitate Christ in their lives.)

10. Isolate one or two truths you've discovered about yourself and your relationship with God from this chapter.

11. What have you discovered from this chapter that the Bible teaches about:

God's expectations of you?

Others' expectations of you?

Your expectations of others?

Your influence on others?

12. Write "11:1" (from 1 Corinthians 11:1) on the palm of your hand or some other conspicuous place as a reminder this week that you are being watched and imitated. Each time you see it, pray and ask the Holy Spirit to empower you and prompt you regarding what He desires for your life.

SCRIPTURE MEMORY

The reality of the watched life—Matthew 23:2-3
The challenge of the watched life—1 Corinthians 11:1

6. JOB

The Sanctified Mouth

ABIDING PRINCIPLE   Our words are a clear reflection of who we are, but they also affect what we are becoming. As we seek to be conformed to the image of Jesus Christ, controlling our speech is essential.

> *Why, indeed, do we converse and gossip among ourselves when we so seldom part without a troubled conscience?*

—Thomas à Kempis

SNAPSHOT   Scores of books, articles, and sermons have been written and preached about the suffering and patience of Job. But most of our insights about Job are essentially confined to the book that bears his name. In fact, he is mentioned by name only three other times in the entire Bible! About six centuries before Christ, in a final statement through the prophet Ezekiel, God reaffirmed Job's character as one whose heart was right before the Lord. The book of Job is essentially a record of conversations among Job, several men, Satan, and God. And while it is true that his patience and faith provide a great model for us to imitate, it is also true that the book and life of Job can teach us a great deal about God's desire to sanctify the speech of those who claim to know Him.

SCRIPTURE   Job 29

1. Job 29 provides an excellent portrayal of Job's past—that portion of his life about which God declared, "There is no one on earth like him; he is blameless and upright, a man who fears God and shuns evil" (Job 1:8; 2:3). Read the following verses from Job 29 and describe Job's life in terms of what he said and what he did.

Verses 11-12

Verse 13

Verse 15

Verse 16

Verses 21-23

Verse 25

2. Job 27:1-4 gives us a glimpse of his convictions after he had been robbed of his peace, his possessions, and even the lives of

his children. What was his commitment concerning his speech in the midst of his suffering and loss? Explain why this is so significant.

3. Job's friends were convinced that his calamity was clearly God's judgment for sin in his life. Contrast the effect of what they said with what Job said concerning his suffering, according to Job 16:1-2 and 19:2.

4. Describe the principle about our speech outlined in Proverbs 18:21.

Explain how you see this principle illustrated in the life of Job.

5. Scripture makes some astounding assertions about the *seriousness* of our speech. What is the plain message you see in each of the following passages?

Psalm 34:12-13

Isaiah 29:13

Matthew 12:36-37

James 3:2-5

6. Read Matthew 12:34-35 and Proverbs 16:23. What principles about our speech do you discover from these passages?

Thoughtfully read Psalm 119:9-11, Proverbs 7:1-3, and Colossians 3:16. What additional insights can you add to your answer to the previous question?

RECAP

In Ezekiel 14:20 God indicates that Job was one of the most upright men who ever lived. And in the book that bears his name we see not only how he responded to an avalanche of suffering that God allowed and ordained, but also how he handled being wrongly accused by his close companions. And through it all, even though some of his reasoning was wrong, Job's speech was faultless before God. The Bible portrays our mouth as the exit ramp of the *heart*. What we say reflects who we are. For this reason, God places a very high premium on our *speech*. In fact, the relationship between our heart and our mouth is so close that at the Day of Judgment our *words* will be the evidence used to describe the condition of our hearts! So if we are being conformed to the likeness of Christ (being sanctified), our speech should clearly be changing; the reflection of what is happening to our hearts.

APPLICATION QUESTIONS

7. Following is a list of Scriptures that deal with different aspects of our speech. Read each one and explain the main point, including both positive and negative instruction.

Deuteronomy 6:6-7

Psalm 40:10

Psalm 141:3

Psalm 141:5

Proverbs 9:8

Proverbs 10:19

Proverbs 12:18

Proverbs 15:1

Proverbs 17:27

Proverbs 29:1

Isaiah 50:4

Ezekiel 2:6-8

Ephesians 4:29

Ephesians 5:4

Ephesians 5:19-20

Colossians 4:6

1 Peter 3:15

8. Prayerfully review your responses to question 7. Choose two areas in which you are not glorifying God in your speech. Put a star next to those verses. Write them out on an index card and plan to memorize them this week. Find a friend or family member who will hold you accountable to this application, and give that person permission to remind you of your commitment to change your speech when he or she hears you sin.

9. Consider your conversations this past week. In the following subject areas, what would people (your friends, family, coworkers, and such) conclude is in your heart, based on what they heard you say? List examples when you can.

God's character

Your relationship with God

Someone who has hurt you

Your level of contentment

What you believe about gossip

_____

What you believe about God's sovereignty

_____

Your feelings toward family members

_____

Your feelings toward coworkers

_____

10. Review your responses to question 9. What is one area in which you would like to see God change your heart and your speech? Prayerfully, write a plan of action, and share it with a trusted friend who will faithfully pray for you and hold you accountable.

SCRIPTURE MEMORY

The tongue's guide—Proverbs 16:23
Sanctified speech—Ephesians 4:29

7. REHOBOAM

Two Models of Leadership

ABIDING PRINCIPLE   One of the most obvious indicators of our maturity in sanctification is our treatment of others—especially of those who are subordinate to us.

A Christian man is the most free, lord of all, and subject to none; he is also the most dutiful servant to all and subject to everyone.

—Martin Luther

SNAPSHOT   Before powerful rulers die, a frenzied power struggle often occurs among those who fancy themselves to be the next in line. Intrigue and conspiracy marked the inner workings of the royal family of King David until Solomon was declared by his father to be his lawful successor. Solomon's own passing, though not marked by the same chaos, signaled the end of a united kingdom. His son Rehoboam, in his first significant decision as successor-king, stands forever in the pages of Scripture as an example of how not to lead. Though well within the circumference of the sovereignty of God, one significant decision was responsible for the division of the nation of Israel into two separate kingdoms. And the consequences of Rehoboam's rejection of wise counselors have persisted for nearly three thousand years! His life story, though brief, is rich with insight for those of us seeking to emulate the One into whose likeness we are being changed. All of us are leading someone—perhaps as parents, or at a job, or maybe just because of our age. Someone is taking his or her lead from our lives.

SCRIPTURE   1 Kings 11:40–12:24

1. Solomon is often eulogized as a man of great wisdom, wealth, and influence. Few however, are aware of some of the *means* he employed to expand his elaborate "portfolio." Explain how he built his resume from the following 1 Kings passages. What did Solomon do as a leader?

4:7

5:1-14

6:37-38

7:1-9

Read 1 Samuel 8:7-20 (a prophecy) and 1 Kings 12:1-4. Explain how these passages either support or contradict the portrait above.

2. Would you consider the request made by Jeroboam's messenger to Solomon's son reasonable (1 Kings 12:4)? Explain your answer.

3. In this story, the new king and novice leader makes some unwise choices. Read 1 Kings 12:1-24 again. Make a list of decisions Rehoboam made that were wise and sound, and a list of decisions that proved to be unwise and foolish.

Evidence of Wise Leadership   Evidence of Unwise Leadership

4. How do you explain the counsel that Rehoboam's childhood friends gave him in verses 8-11? (Note: The words translated "grown up with him" mean that they rose to power with him. They too were children of nobility.)

5. Someone has differentiated between power and authority this way: *Power* is the ability to get people to do what you ask because they are afraid of the consequences if they don't. *Authority* is the ability to get people to do what you ask because they respect you and believe the request is reasonable. Using this principle as a guide, and the story of Rehoboam as a case study, answer the following questions. (You may need to refer to 1 Kings 12:3-16.)

State which leadership model (power or authority) you think takes the greater amount of time and effort, and explain why.

How do you think a new leader can lead by authority if he is relatively unfamiliar with the people he is leading?

Why do you think the elders counseled Rehoboam to "be a servant to these people and serve them and give them a favorable answer, [so] they will always be [his] servants"?

How was their counsel actually an opportunity for Rehoboam to establish the means to lead by authority? (Think carefully!)

Which model—power or authority—is preferred by leaders? (Think of yourself leading, and of other leaders.) Explain your answer.

Which of the two models requires a higher standard of integrity? Explain.

6. Read Isaiah 55:1–56:7 and Hosea 11:1-9. Which model of leadership does God exhibit here? Explain your answer.

7. God has the right to lead us by power, and often people relate to Him that way. Yet He prefers to lead by authority. Why do you think it is easier to lead when the power model is exercised?

Why do we find it easier to *follow* when we are being led by the authority model?

8. Review your responses in this section and write a brief summary of what you've discovered about leadership from this chapter in terms of both leaders and followers.

Leaders

Followers

RECAP

Leaders have followers. They may be appointed by popular choice, or rise to power through deceit and a desire to control. But they cannot successfully lead unless those under them are willing to follow. There is a difference between leading and herding people, even though there is a movement or progress associated with both methods. Leading by intimidation and threat of punishment is easier, takes less time, and does not demand integrity. It also kindles the natural rebellion that resides deep in the hearts of those required to obey. People led by this method spend their time searching for an escape route, or the end of the leader's reign. God does not lead His people this way. He may lovingly discipline us for disobedience, but He always longs for us to follow Him out of a heart of trust and love, never fear of future pain.

APPLICATION QUESTIONS

9. Read Mark 10:31-45; this summarizes everything that you discovered in the first section of this chapter. What does Jesus say about the two models of leadership and the person who wants to follow Him?

What does He say about His own life and this issue?

10. If sanctification is the ongoing process of being conformed to the likeness of Jesus Christ, why do we need to take this issue of leadership style seriously?

11. Each of the following passages contains a principle about servant leadership Jesus taught His disciples. Explain each principle and then finish the sentence as personally as possible.

John 13:1-17

In light of this truth I need to . . .

John 21:1-12

In light of this truth I need to . . .

1 Corinthians 11:1

In light of this truth I need to . . .

Galatians 5:22-23

In light of this truth I need to . . .

Ephesians 6:7-9

In light of this truth I need to . . .

1 Thessalonians 2:6-12

In light of this truth I need to . . .

2 Timothy 2:24-26

In light of this truth I need to . . .

Hebrews 13:7,17

In light of this truth I need to . . .

12. Not all "leadership" is planned and formal, and most of us are leading more frequently than we realize. Any relationship in which someone looks to you for direction, instruction, or boundaries is one in which you have a leadership role. (The person looking to you might even be a peer.) Make a list of all the relationships in your life right now in which you play a leadership role.

13. Using this chapter as a guide, review your list from the previous question to determine whether you are leading by power or authority in each of the relationships you listed. Mark a relationship with a "P" if you think you are leading that person through the principle of *power* (fear of punishment or consequences); mark a relationship with an "A" for *authority* if you are seeking to lead that person by living as a servant.

14. Look at the relationships on your list you marked with an "A." Would you say your leadership style is the product of biblical convictions about how God wants you to lead, or the result of your personal feelings about the person you are leading? Explain your answer.

15. Answer the same question for the relationships on your list you marked with a "P."

16. Explain what you have learned from this chapter about yourself that is reflected in the way you relate to those you lead.

17. Commit to make two biblical changes in the way you lead with relationships in your life right now. Share your discovery and intent with a trusted friend. Ask your friend to pray for you daily for two weeks while you seek to implement the necessary changes by the enabling power of God's Spirit.

SCRIPTURE MEMORY

Two methods of leadership—Matthew 20:25-28
Jesus' model of leadership—Mark 10:45

8. THE UNJUST STEWARD

Dollars and Sense

ABIDING PRINCIPLE   Our perspective on wealth and possessions affects not only the direction of our lives, but often our
destination.

*The truly rich man is not he who has the most, but the one
who needs the least.*

—Unknown

SNAPSHOT   God meticulously orchestrated the composition of
the Bible. Prophets, poets, and preachers contribute to our
understanding of the nature and character of God and man. And
in the Bible, His plans and purposes for our lives unfold. Some of
the most profound teaching in Scripture comes from the most
unexpected sources; we are admonished to learn from ants, fish,
and fowl! God also wants us to discover truth from the disobe-
dient people as well as those who followed Him with a heart of
love. One such negative teacher, in a story recorded only in
Luke's gospel, is known simply as "the unjust steward." His perspective on money and possessions cost him his reputation and
his occupation. Yet deep within this story is not only a principle
about wealth that explains the steward's demise, but also a sober
warning about the crucial need to have a godly view of money
and possessions.

SCRIPTURE   Luke 16:1-15

1. Because this parable appears at first glance to be paradoxical, it will be best to build an understanding of the story itself. There is one major point. Look at the verses associated with each question below. In your own words, thoughtfully reconstruct the story.

Luke 16:1—What was the actual charge brought against the steward by his employer? (Note: The word translated "wasting" in this verse is the same as the word translated "squandered" in Luke 15:13, referring to what the younger son did with his inheritance.)

In modern terminology, what do you think the steward was doing?

2. Luke 16:3-4—What becomes the steward's goal once he realizes that he's about to be "out in the street"?

Luke 16:4-7—How does the steward plan to achieve his goal? (Note: The word "quickly" is very important, and the "bill" here was like a contract.)

3. Comparing verses 1-2 with verse 8, how do you explain the obvious fact that the employer was impressed with the person he was about to fire?

4. The key to this passage and parable is found in verse 9. The word translated "gain" (NIV) or "make" (KJV, NASB) can mean to construct or craft something. What is Jesus telling His disciples and us about the primary purpose of worldly wealth?

The words for "wealth" and "money" in verses 9,11, and 13 are all the same. But in verse 13 we discover a principle about money that provides greater meaning to the story of the unjust steward. What does Jesus say about the believer and money in this verse?

5. It has been said that money is either a tool or an idol. Do your responses in question 4 support or contradict this statement? Explain your answer.

Does your assessment agree or disagree with Luke 12:34? Explain.

6. Read Matthew 19:16-24 several times. This short encounter contains the record of one man's attempt to love both God and wealth. He walked away sad when he was told that the way to eternal life conflicted with his comfortable lifestyle. Explain what you see in the young man's life that illustrates the point in each of the following passages.

Matthew 6:19-21

Matthew 6:24

Matthew 22:34-40

1 Timothy 6:6-10

7. In Ezekiel 28:1-5, God is speaking to His own people who believed that financial gain was evidence of the blessing of God. Do the prophet's words support their belief? Explain your answer.

8. Read Job 1:1-3 and Job 1:13-21. What was Job's view of God and the wealth that He had entrusted to him?

In Luke 8:1-3 we read about several women who were followers of Jesus. What was their vision for the financial resources that God had entrusted to them?

RECAP

God says repeatedly in Scripture that riches wage an effective warfare for the hearts of people. Wealth can be deceptive, temporary, and arid. It enslaves more often than it emancipates. Yet we read of people like Abraham, David, Job, and Susanna who had great wealth and walked intimately with God. They had learned the truth that wealth is either a tool or an idol. Wealth either serves us as we serve Him, or we serve it, seeking to serve ourselves. There is no middle ground. In short, what we *do* with our money and possessions is the result of how we view them.

APPLICATION QUESTIONS

9. The subject of money and possessions is a prominent and persistent theme in the Bible. Unfortunately, our own convictions on the subject are often the result of common sense rather than careful study of God's Word. Look up each of the following verses and formulate a concise but clear principle about your own money and its relationship to your spiritual life.

Leviticus 25:35-37

Deuteronomy 8:17-18

Psalm 62:10

Proverbs 23:5

Ecclesiastes 5:10-11

Ecclesiastes 5:19

Matthew 13:22

Mark 10:23-27

Luke 12:34

Luke 16:11

1 Timothy 6:9-10

James 2:5

Revelation 3:17

10. The Bible not only provides instruction and insight regarding our relationship to money and possessions, it also enlightens our understanding of true riches, investing, and spending. Read the following passages and construct a one- or two-sentence principle the Bible teaches about true wealth, wise investing, and spending.

Psalm 119:14,72,127

Proverbs 11:24

2 Corinthians 6:10

2 Corinthians 8:13-14

2 Corinthians 9:6-7

2 Corinthians 9:10-13

Ephesians 3:8

2 Peter 3:10-13

11. Look over your responses to questions 9 and 10. Summarize two or three areas in which your view of money and wealth has changed because of what you have discovered in this study.

12. Think about your own use of the financial resources God has entrusted to you. In light of how you actually live (how you spend your money, what you spend your money on, and so on), what would people, including family members, say your convictions are in the following areas?

Your possessions (private ownership vs. stewardship of what belongs to God)

Your possessions (tools to be used vs. gifts to be enjoyed)

Your money (used for things that perish vs. used for people, who live forever)

Your money (a percentage belongs to God vs. all belongs to God)

Your money (enables personal comfort vs. empowers personal ministry)

13. How are your perspective and lifestyle regarding money and possessions the *same* as an unbeliever's? (Be honest!)

How are they *different?*

14. What is one thing you can do to change your perspective on your possessions?

Your money?

Who will hold you accountable to do this? Write down that person's name and decide what you will ask him or her to do to help you.

Read Luke 6:38. What is the promise in this passage about true giving and true wealth?

SCRIPTURE MEMORY

The dangers of wealth—Hosea 13:6
The purpose of wealth—1 Timothy 6:17-19

9. PAUL

The Power of Contentment

ABIDING PRINCIPLE   The genuineness of our contentment is perhaps the most accurate measure of our understanding and acceptance of God's lovingkindness, competence, and sovereignty.

> *True contentment is a thing as active as agriculture. It is the power of getting out of any situation all that there is in it. It is arduous, and it is rare.*

—G.K. Chesterton

SNAPSHOT   The apostle Paul, more than any other biblical figure, was a man of cosmopolitan experience. In his ministry, he mingled with more ethnic groups, visited more cities, saw a wider range of human emotions, and encountered a greater diversity of thoughts and perspectives than any other person in the pages of God's Word. Paul's life was a punctuated series of vacillating extremes. In one city he was deified and worshiped as an incarnation of a god. In another town he had to be lowered from the city wall in a basket at night to escape imminent death. Exonerated and beaten, esteemed and despised, Paul was well-acquainted with the variegated nature of life. Yet through it all, Paul exhibited a character quality that, perhaps more than any other characteristic, is a barometer of what one really believes about God's love and His sovereignty in our lives—contentment. Its growing presence in our lives indicates progress in sanctification, but its absence is evidence of either a misunderstanding of the gospel or a refusal to surrender the stronghold of self in our lives.

SCRIPTURE   Philippians 4:4-20

1. Paul speaks of contentment in all circumstances in Philippians 4:10-11. Summarize what some of these circumstances were for Paul based on what you find in the following passages.

Acts 16:22-25

Acts 19:8-12

2 Corinthians 1:8-10

2 Corinthians 7:5-7

2 Corinthians 11:27-28

2 Corinthians 12:7-10

Philippians 4:14-18

2. Read Philippians 1:13-14. Why is it particularly powerful for Paul to extol contentment based on what was going on in his life?

3. Paul's choice of words in Philippians 4:11 is very significant. The word translated "content" is used only here in the New Testament. It is a compound word that basically means to need no outside help or assistance. This idea could be misunderstood or misconstrued to suggest that we are meant to be self-sufficient or independent. Compare Philippians 4:11 with 2 Corinthians 12:9 and Philippians 4:13. What further understanding about contentment do you gain from Paul in these verses?

Contentment for Paul meant . . .

4. Carefully read Hebrews 13:5 several times. This verse portrays contentment as arising from our choice to focus on one thing in the midst of everything that we have. What is it?

How do you think that this can produce contentment in *all* circumstances?

5. A sobering principle about contentment is contained in two Old Testament passages that deal with the failure of the Israelites in this area. Summarize the central truth regarding contentment and lack of contentment contained in these verses.

Exodus 16:8

6. What does Colossians 3:5 teach about the absence of contentment and its impact on one's relationship with God? Look carefully!

7. Paul makes a very powerful connection between contentment (or the lack of it) and our sanctification in Philippians 2:12-15. Why is it significant that his comments in verse 14 follow right on the heels of what he says about God in the previous verse?

RECAP

Paul, writing from prison, said he had come to the place in his life where he had been initiated into something that not everyone knew or even believed. He claimed that he understood that true contentment was the result of trusting fully in God's sufficiency. He also had confidence that the greater his need, the greater God's provision. Consequently, he was able to be "content" in all circumstances because he could do all things through Christ's strength. Contentment is the conviction that what we have is enough because we have God Himself. If His grace is sufficient and His presence is permanent, we do possess everything in every circumstance. When we are dissatisfied and desire more, we are by definition assuming that He has become less. Finally, the true contentment that we seek is inseparably bound to our progress in godliness—sanctification.

APPLICATION QUESTIONS

8. Below is a sampling of areas in which all of us struggle with contentment. Describe how these verses might apply to your own life.

Proverbs 19:3

Matthew 6:31-32

Luke 3:14

Luke 8:14

Luke 12:15

Romans 12:3-8

Galatians 1:10

1 Timothy 6:6-8

James 1:2-4

9. Discontent is never quiet or still. In fact, its clearest expression is addressed repeatedly in the Bible. In the Old Testament, the word is translated "murmuring" or "grumbling." The majority of times the word is used, it refers to "camping" or "lodging" somewhere (see Numbers 17:5 and Numbers 22:8). In your own words, explain how we are "lodging" or "camping" on an issue when we grumble or complain.

10. In the New Testament, one of the words translated "grumbling" or "murmuring" actually refers to the sound made by doves cooing or bees buzzing. It is typically employed when groups of people are conferring or talking among themselves, like the Pharisees in Luke 5:30 or Jesus' audience in John 6:41-43. Why do you think discontent and grumbling thrives in group situations?

11. Carefully examine the following passages of Scripture. They describe the thoughts of people who are content. Describe why you think the person in each verse is content. Begin each of your answers with the phrase, "Contentment dwells in the person who . . ."

Psalm 4:7

Psalm 34:1

Psalm 63:3

Psalm 73:21-26

Psalm 119:69-70

Proverbs 15:16

Isaiah 26:3

Colossians 3:15-17

What have you discovered from these verses regarding your own struggles with contentment? What needs to change? What will you do to begin this change?

12. Write out 1 Timothy 6:6 below.

Underline the two things that Paul says should go together.

Do you think it is possible to have one without the other? Explain your answer.

---

13. Review your responses to question 8. Reflect on your conversations with people (including family) over the past week. How many areas of life have you "camped on" in regard to discontent? Put a star by the ones that you have "murmured" about to someone else.

---

14. Look at your responses to question 11. Think back again on your conversations over the past week. How would you rate your speech in regard to pointing others to God's goodness to you?

The psalmist ———————————————— Jesus in the
                                                       wilderness

---

15. Prayerfully assess your answers to the last two questions. Select one area where you need to see God develop a heart and tongue of contentment in your life. Enlist a friend or family member who hears you speak frequently to pray for you as you seek to change the way you think and then speak. Ask him or her to faithfully alert you when you begin to "murmur."

Area where I seek God's help to develop contentment

Person (or persons) I will ask to help me

The true "target" of murmuring—Exodus 16:8
Contentment and sanctification—1 Timothy 6:6

10. THE GOOD SAMARITAN

Ministering to the "Least of These"

ABIDING PRINCIPLE   Those whose hearts and minds are being transformed into the likeness of Jesus Christ will discover that they have an increasing interest in the kinds of people He came to seek and to save.

> *The honest poor can sometimes forget poverty. The honest rich can never forget it.*

—G.K. Chesterton

SNAPSHOT   Possibly one of the most well-known characters from the Bible is the "good Samaritan." He has found a permanent place in the world of anecdotes about compassion. It is also rare to find any discussion of this ethereal character without the adjective "good" as a prefix, even though Jesus never made that attribution! Something deep within us seems to demand that this Samaritan man be christened "good." We instinctively sense that what *he* is, we should be. Yet this story is robbed of its original impact because we cannot appreciate how offensive it would have been to those who first heard it. The Jews of Jesus' day would not have seen this Samaritan's act as one of selfless service. Instead, it would have been received as a howling reproach. And one of the most significant aspects of this entire account is often overlooked: In telling this parable, Jesus gives us a glimpse into His own heart. And for those of us who are seeking to cooperate with His Father in molding us into His image, this story should have a sacred place.

SCRIPTURE   2 Kings 17:1-24; Luke 10:25-37

1. Look carefully at the question-and-answer exchange that Jesus had with the "lawyer" ("expert in the law," NIV) in Luke 10:25-29. Use this passage to answer the following questions.

What was the lawyer asking Jesus?

Jesus makes the lawyer answer his own question in verses 26-28. What are the two requirements for eternal life?

1.

2.

Based on the lawyer's final question, in verse 29, what must he be assuming about his own life and the first of these two requirements?

2. Jesus' intention in this story is to lead the lawyer to discover that he does not truly love God. He does this subtly but firmly. The skillful rebuke is in the change of questions that Jesus brings about. Look at the lawyer's original question (verse 29) and Jesus' final question (verse 36). What did Jesus accomplish by so artfully changing the focus?

The stinging rebuke in this parable is the choice of Jesus to use a Samaritan as the champion. In order to understand the impact of the parable, we need to understand the history of the Samaritans and their relationship to the Jews of Jesus' day. Read 2 Kings 17:1-24 and answer these questions.

Verses 1-2 Who is inhabiting the area known as Samaria in these verses?

Verses 3-17 What characterized the behavior of these Jews?

Verses 18-23 What did God do to His people and how did He accomplish it?

Verse 24 What did the Assyrian king do after removing the Jews from Samaria?

3. These non-Jews intermarried with the Jews who were allowed to remain. Over the next several hundred years they eventually built their own temple on Mount Gerazim in Samaria and established their own system of worship. Hostility and hatred grew. What can you glean about the Samaritans and Jews from the encounter Jesus had with a Samaritan woman in John 4:2-42? (As you read this account, keep in mind that the conflict in this story is nearly seven hundred years old!)

Verse 12

Verse 20

John 4:25

___

John 4:9

___

Luke 9:51-54

___

4. What effect does this have on your understanding of how the parable of the good Samaritan would have been received by the lawyer and those listening?

___

Has this changed your understanding of Jesus' main point in this parable? Explain.

___

5. This parable is also a summary of the life and ministry of Jesus. He too was "despised and rejected by men" (Isaiah 53:3) and did "not come to call the righteous, but sinners" (Mark 2:17). If we are to become like Him, it is important that we know what the people were like who He ministered to and associated with. We need to know what Jesus said and what He did. Read the following passages and describe who Jesus ministered to and why it was significant.

___

Matthew 9:10-13 (see also Luke 18:13)

Matthew 19:13-14

Mark 5:24-34 (see also Leviticus 15:25-27)

Luke 4:16-21

Luke 5:12-13 (see also Leviticus 13:43-46)

Luke 7:21

Luke 7:36-47

Luke 8:27-37

RECAP

To first-century Jews, the parable of the good Samaritan could
have been perceived as a condemnation of their religious beliefs.

In a typical turn of events, Jesus elevated the enemy of the story to the status of a hero. In so doing, He rebuked the Jews for their hardness of heart toward others and toward Him. But His message has modern implications too. A brief study of the life and ministry of Jesus reveals an attraction to the people in society who are often overlooked or judged, even in our own day. Jesus' command to the lawyer, "Go and do likewise," should echo in our own ears and hearts as we enter into the flow of humanity that exists in the world around us each day.

APPLICATION QUESTIONS

6. Read Matthew 18:23-35. There is a profound principle in this parable that actually explains what should be at the heart of a Christian's willingness and desire to meet the needs of people. How is this parable related to the parable of the good Samaritan?

7. Jeremiah 24:7 contains one of the most exciting promises in the Bible. What is God's promise here and what do you think it means?

Look at Jeremiah 22:16. Compare it with 24:7 and your response above. What is the relationship between these two verses?

8. Read Isaiah 58:5-10. In this passage, God reveals what a truly religious and spiritual person does who is seeking to worship Him in an acceptable way. What is the relationship between these verses and what you've learned in the study so far?

Has what you've learned challenged the ideas you had about ministry when you began this study? If so, what are some changes that you will make?

9. Review your answers to question 5. In the following chart, write a one- or two-word description of the kinds of people Jesus was ministering to in the "Then" column. In the column marked "Now," explain who would be an equivalent people group in our world today.

Then	Now

10. In Matthew 25:31-46, Jesus makes a sobering statement about the relationship between ministry to others and judgment. While theologians debate significant points of interpretation in this passage, a number of truths are inescapable. Read the passage carefully and then answer the following questions.

What are the six categories of needy people Jesus mentions in this passage?

1   4.

2.   5.

3.   6.

What phrase does Jesus use in verses 40 and 45 to describe these people?

What added identification does Jesus attach to these people in verse 40 that is significantly different from the other people groups you've studied in this chapter so far?

Think of who these people are in your world. *Who* are they and *where* are they?

How many of them are you ministering to? (If you have no ministry with any of these people, you may need to repent of your negligence, and perhaps repent of any prejudices you may have about people Jesus Himself called "brothers of mine.")

11. As you come to the end of this Bible study, perhaps this chapter more than any of the others has revealed your willingness or unwillingness to cooperate with God in the process of making you more like His Son. Take a few minutes right now to consider who the "least of these" are in your city, Christians and unbelievers alike. How can you minister to "Jesus" in a way that is consistent with what you've learned in this chapter and this study? Write a short paragraph explaining what you will do. You may want to discuss this with your small group, a Sunday school class, or with the

members of your family. Perhaps you can begin to get involved with a phone call or a letter to an individual or agency working with the people groups Jesus sought out when He was on earth. The larger truth is, He is still on earth . . . and *we* are His Body.

SCRIPTURE MEMORY

Knowing God means meeting needs—Jeremiah 22:16
Compassion to the oppressed—Matthew 25:40